First Lessons Music Theory

by Katherine Curatolo

© 2013 BY MEL BAY PUBLICATIONS, INC., PACIFIC, MO 63069.
ALL RIGHTS RESERVED. INTERNATIONAL COPYRIGHT SECURED. B.M.I. MADE AND PRINTED IN U.S.A.
No part of this publication may be reproduced in whole or in part, or stored in a retrieval system, or transmitted in any form
or by any means, electronic, mechanical, photocopy, recording, or otherwise, without written permission of the publisher.

Visit us on the Web at www.melbay.com — E-mail us at email@melbay.com

Introduction

This book is an introduction to music theory. The twenty-six lessons start from the beginning with a guide to reading a music staff and progress to providing an explanation of topics ranging from rhythm to different kinds of chords. By the end of this book, the reader will be familiar with all of the terms and concepts necessary for a basic and confident understanding of music.

With deep gratitude, I acknowledge Kyle Masson for generously providing editorial assistance and invaluable suggestions for the revision of this manuscript.

Table of Contents

Lesson 1:	The Staff	4
Lesson 2:	Quarter, Half, Whole Notes and Rests	6
Lesson 3:	Time Signature	7
Lesson 4:	Key Signature	8
Lesson 5:	8th, 16th, 32nd Notes and Rests	9
Lesson 6:	Rhythm	12
Lesson 7:	Dotted Notes	13
Lesson 8:	Dotted Rhythms	14
Lesson 9:	Accidentals	15
Lesson 10:	Enharmonic Notes	16
Lesson 11:	Intervals	17
Lesson 12:	Order of Sharps and Flats	19
Lesson 13:	Major Keys	20
Lesson 14:	Scale Degrees	21
Lesson 15:	Major Scale	22
Lesson 16:	Triplets	23
Lesson 17:	Dynamics and Articulations	24
Lesson 18:	Repeats	25
Lesson 19:	More Time Signatures	26
Lesson 20:	Tempo	27
Lesson 21:	Minor Keys	28
Lesson 22:	Minor Scales	29
Lesson 23:	Triads	30
Lesson 24:	Arpeggios	32
Lesson 25:	Inversions	33
Lesson 26:	Seventh Chords	34

Lesson 1
The Staff

Music is written on a **staff**. The first step in learning to read music is to understand the staff and its parts.

The staff consists of five lines and four spaces. At the beginning of the staff, there is a symbol called a **clef**.

To the right of the clef on the staff is the **key signature**, which is a collection of symbols describing the **key** of the music. There will not always be a visible key signature.

To the right of the key signature is the **time signature**, which describes how to count the music. It consists of two stacked numbers.

In this book, the clef used is a **treble clef**, also known as a **G clef**. Some of the instruments that use treble clef are guitar, flute, and violin. Other instruments read music using different clefs. Here are some examples:

Bass clef (bass guitar, cello, tuba):   C clef (viola):

𝄢   𝄡

Written music will not always look exactly as it has been described here so far. It changes depending on which and how many instruments are reading the music. For example, piano music is written on the **grand staff**, which has two staffs, one for each hand. The top staff is written in treble clef and the bottom staff in bass clef.

The staff is divided into **measures**, which are indicated by **barlines**. Measures represent divisions of musical time. At the end of a piece of music, there is a final bar line called a **double bar line**.

Notes are written on the lines or in the spaces of the staff. The round part of the note is called the **notehead** and the line attached to it is called the **stem**. When a note falls above or below the boundaries of the staff, it is written on a **ledger line**.

Each note, or pitch, has a letter name. The notes are: A, B, C, D, E, F, G.

In **treble clef**, the notes on the lines are, from bottom to top, **E, G, B, D, F**. To remember this, memorize the sentence "**E**very **G**ood **B**oy **D**oes **F**ine".

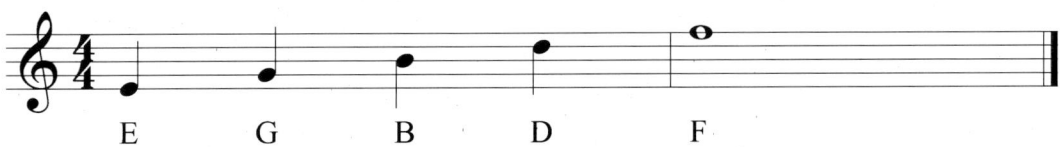

The notes in the spaces, from bottom to top, are **F, A, C, E**. These letters are easy to remember because they spell the word "Face".

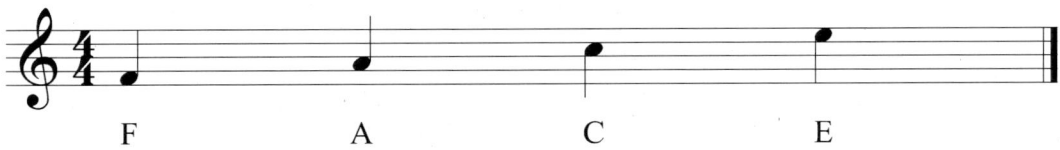

A line of notes in order is called a **scale**. An **octave** is a distance of eight notes. A one-octave scale is comprised of eight notes, beginning and ending on the same letter-named note, one octave apart. Below is a one-octave scale in the key of C major, ascending and descending.

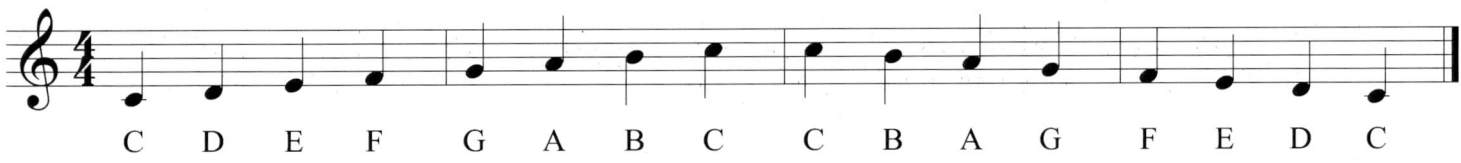

Memorizing the placement of the notes on the staff is the key to reading music fluently. Study the above examples until recognizing the location of the notes becomes second-nature.

Lesson 2
Quarter, Half, Whole Notes and Rests

Different kinds of notes represent different amounts of time in music. In the 4/4 time signature, there are four beats in a measure and a quarter note equals one beat.

Each type of note has a corresponding **rest** sign. A **rest** is a period of silence in music and has a set time length that matches the note to which it corresponds. When there is a rest in a piece of music, do not play or sing for the amount of musical time the rest represents. In the example below, the symbols in the second measure are **quarter note rests**. Each time there is a quarter note rest, refrain from playing or singing for the duration of one quarter note.

A **half note** equals two beats (or two quarter notes). It looks like a quarter note with a hollow notehead. A **half note rest** also lasts for two beats and sits on top of the middle line on the staff.

A **whole note** equals four beats (equal to two half notes or four quarter notes). It is hollow and has no stem. A **whole note rest** hangs below the middle line on the staff and also lasts for four beats.

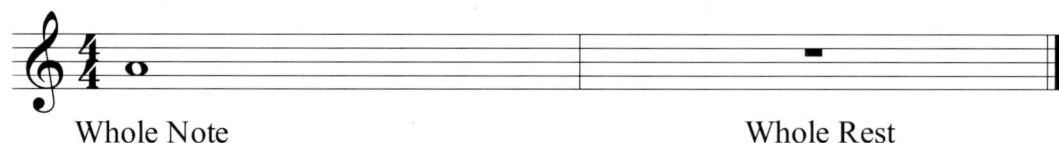

The example below combines whole notes, half notes, and quarter notes. Try clapping or tapping the notes while counting out loud, using the numbers below the staff as a guide.

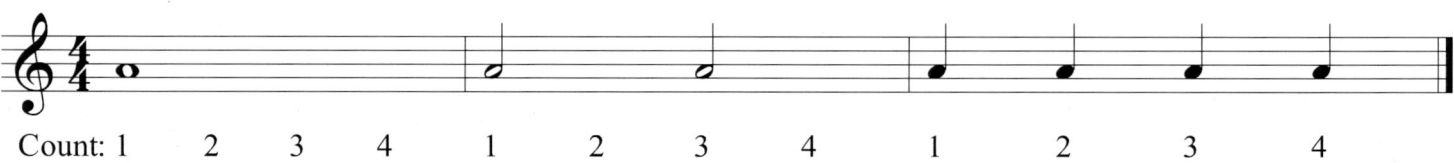

Lesson 3
Time Signature

The **time signature** is a set of two numbers that describe how to count a piece of music. The top number is the number of beats in a measure, and the bottom number is the kind of note that equals, or "gets," a beat. A **beat** is one count.

In **4/4 time**, the top number tells us that there are four beats in a measure and the bottom number indicates that the quarter note "gets the beat". In other words, the measure is counted in quarter notes and there are four quarter notes in the measure.

Because 4/4 time is used frequently, sometimes it is called **common time**. The symbol for common time is a large letter "C". When you see the common time symbol at the beginning of the piece of music, know that the music is in 4/4 time.

Here are some examples of other time signatures counted in quarter notes:

In **2/4 time**, there are two beats in a measure and the quarter note gets the beat.

In **3/4 time**, there are three beats in a measure and the quarter note gets the beat.

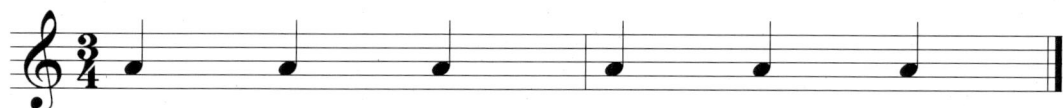

There are many different possible time signatures, and sometimes the time signature changes in the middle of the music. Once you know how to read and understand time signatures, you will be able to count music.

Lesson 4
Key Signature

The **key** of a piece of music describes how the notes should be played or sung in terms of pitch. The same letter-named note changes pitch, or tone, depending on whether it is sharp or flat.

Sharps (♯) and **flats** (♭) are symbols that change the pitch of a note. A sharp raises the pitch one half-step and a flat lowers the pitch one half-step. A **half-step** is a type of **interval**, or distance between notes.

In the examples below, notice how sharp and flat symbols look in different key signatures.

Sharps (Key: D major)   Flats (Key: E flat major)

In a given key, certain notes will always be sharp or flat unless indicated otherwise. The **key signature** tells us which notes are sharp or flat. It will have anywhere from zero to seven sharps or flats. Each key has a specific number of sharps or flats in its key signature.

The key signature at the beginning of the music and at the start of each additional line tells us which notes are sharp or flat, and we have to remember this information throughout the music. Individual notes will not be marked with sharp or flat symbols from the key signature; if a note is sharp or flat in the key signature then it will be sharp or flat each time we come across it in the music.

In the example below, the key signature is for the key of A major, which has three sharps: F, C, and G. Study the labels: even though none of the individual notes in the scale are marked with sharp symbols, the notes marked as sharp in the key signature are sharp in the music.

A   B   C♯   D   E   F♯   G♯   A

Lesson 5
8th, 16th, 32nd Notes and Rests

On this page, we will explore notes that are fractions of a quarter note, or notes that have a time value of less than one beat in time signatures where the quarter note gets the beat.

An **eighth note** equals half of a beat. Two eighth notes equal one quarter note. An eighth note looks like a quarter note with a **flag** attached to the stem. When there are two or more eighth notes in a row, they are often connected by a **beam**. In the example below, the new symbols are **eighth note rests** and last for half a beat each.

When counting eighth notes out loud, the second half of each beat can be spoken as "and": "1 and 2 and 3 and 4 and". Speak and clap the example below.

Now clap the example below, which includes eighth rests. Only clap the notes.

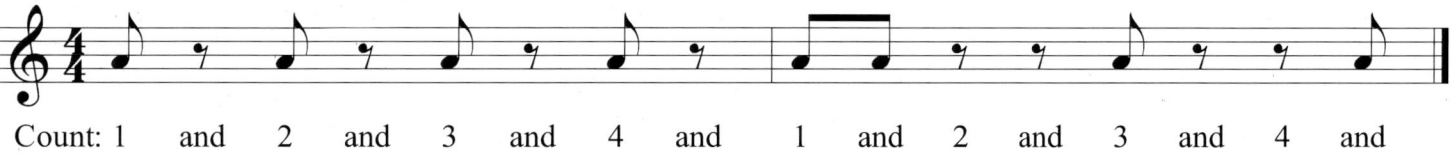

A **sixteenth note** equals one quarter of a beat and one half of an eighth note. Four sixteenth notes equal one quarter note. A sixteenth note looks like an eighth note with two flags on its stem. When two sixteenth notes occur in a row, they are often connected by a **double beam**. A **sixteenth rest** looks like an eighth note rest with an extra flag. In the example below, notice how the different kinds of notes fit together in a measure with four beats.

Count consecutive sixteenth notes out loud by saying "one-e-and-a". A measure of 4/4 time would be counted: "1-e-and-a, 2-e-and-a, 3-e-and-a, 4-e-and-a". Speak and clap the example below:

Now clap and count the following example, which includes sixteenth note rests. In many cases, more than one 16th rest in a row will be condensed into an 8th rest. Just as there are two 16th notes in an 8th note, there are two 16th rests in an 8th rest. Remember that a quarter rest equals one beat, and notice how different types of rests fit together in the example below. Clap only on the notes; rests are silent.

A **32nd** note equals one half of a sixteenth note. There are two 32nd notes in a sixteenth note and eight 32nd notes in a quarter note. A 32nd note has three flags on its stem, and multiple 32nd notes in a row may be connected by a triple beam. A **32nd rest** looks like an eighth note rest with three flags.

32nd notes can be counted verbally in the same way as 16th notes ("one-e-and-a"), only twice as fast and with twice as many notes in a measure. Count and clap the following example slowly; the goal is to understand how the notes fit into four beats.

Count: 1   2   3   4

Next, clap and count the example below, which combines 32nd notes with rests of various durations. As you count the rests, silently think a steady stream of 32nd notes; this will help make clear how to count the beats. Silently "thinking beats" while counting through rests or longer notes is called **subdivision** and is a good habit to develop for when music gets more complex.

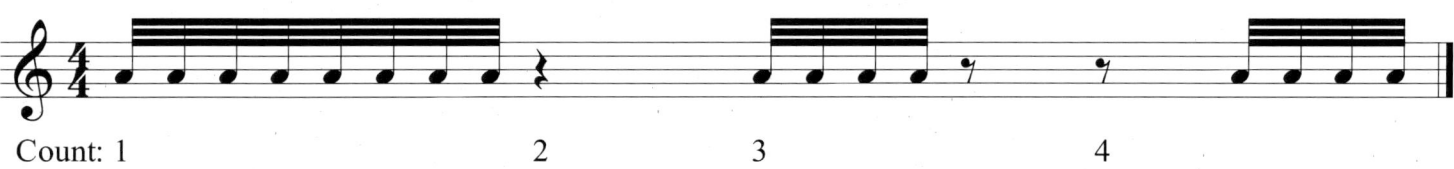

Count: 1   2   3   4

The next example shows the kinds of notes introduced in this lesson. Notice how many of each note type add up to a full measure.

11

Lesson 6
Rhythm

Rhythm is the division of time within music. Having a good sense of rhythm means being aware of the **pulse**, or where the beats fall. It is important to become comfortable enough with counting music to be able to internalize, or feel, the pulse. With enough practice and use of a metronome, you will develop a strong sense of rhythm. This will allow you to always play or sing in time.

The exercises on this page combine the kinds of notes introduced so far into different rhythmic patterns. Set a metronome at 60 beats per minute (bpm) and clap or tap the notes while counting out loud, using the numbered beats under the music as a guide. If 60 bpm is too fast, start more slowly and gradually increase the speed as you become more comfortable counting and clapping the exercises. The goal is to develop the coordination to be able to successfully count and clap simultaneously.

Lesson 7
Dotted Notes

The time value of a note can be increased by adding a dot after the note. Such notes are called **dotted notes**. A dot adds an additional time value of half of the note it follows.

A **dotted half note** is worth three beats. The dot adds one additional beat.

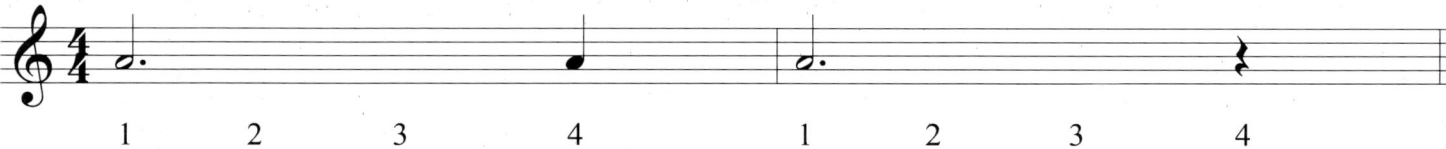

A **dotted quarter note** is worth one and one-half beats. The dot adds the time value of an eighth note. When counting, the dotted quarter note gets two counts, followed by an eighth note that can be counted as "and".

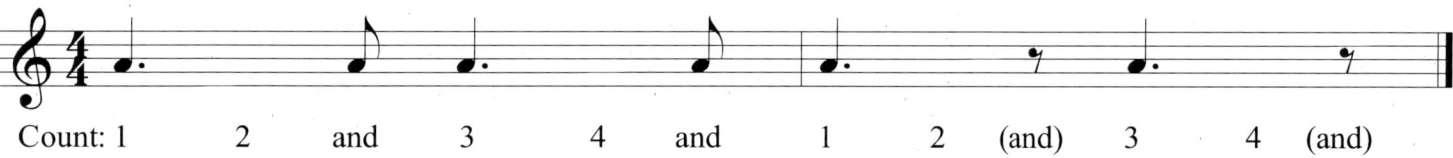

A **dotted eighth note** is worth one and one-half eighth notes, or three sixteenth notes. The dot adds the equivalent of a sixteenth note. When counting this rhythm, it is helpful to think a steady stream of 16th notes. A common rhythm that uses dotted 8th notes is a dotted 8th note followed by a 16th note, shown here connected by a beam.

Rests can be dotted in the same way as notes. In the following example, note the different types of **dotted rests**.

Lesson 8
Dotted Rhythms

The following examples combine the dotted notes and rests introduced in Lesson 7 with the other types of notes and rests discussed earlier. Using a metronome, practice speaking the beats while clapping or tapping the notes until you can fluently do both at once.

The symbol at the end of each line is a **repeat sign**. It has a double bar line with two dots preceding it. When you see a repeat sign, go back to the beginning of the line and clap through the music again.

Lesson 9
Accidentals

We have already seen sharps and flats as part of a key signature, where they tell us which notes will be sharp or flat throughout the music. Sometimes, notes will be different in pitch from what the key signature tells us. These notes are outside of the key and are called **accidentals**. Accidentals are written as **sharp, flat,** or **natural signs** in front of a note. Recall that a **sharp** sign *raises* the pitch by one half-step and a **flat** sign *lowers* the pitch by one half-step. A **natural** sign cancels out a sharp or flat and means to play the note as a basic letter note. An accidental remains in effect for one measure, which means that each time the note occurs in that measure it will be played as though it has that same accidental. The accidental is canceled out before the end of the measure if a different accidental is used in front of that note.

The note "A" with a sharp in front of it is called "A sharp," and with a flat in front of it is called "A flat". A note without a symbol is called "A natural," or just "A". If the note has a natural symbol in front of it, it would also be correct to call it either "A natural" or "A".

Take a look at the example below and name each note. Remember that when an accidental is written it remains in effect for the entire measure or until the note is marked with a different accidental. Check your answers with the answer key provided beneath the exercise.

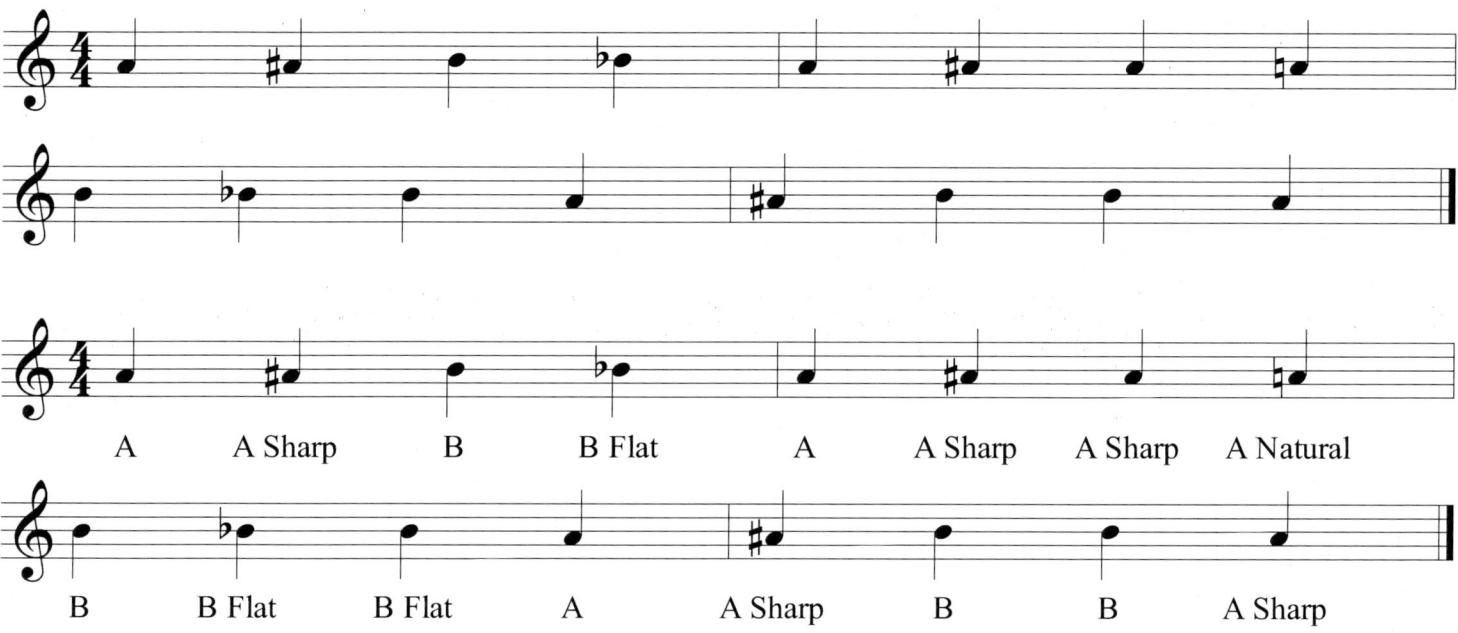

15

Lesson 10
Enharmonic Notes

Enharmonic notes are notes that have the same pitch but different letter names. The key of the music determines which note names are used. The easiest way to understand this concept is to look at the piano keyboard. Below you will see that many of the keys on the piano have more than one note name assigned to them:

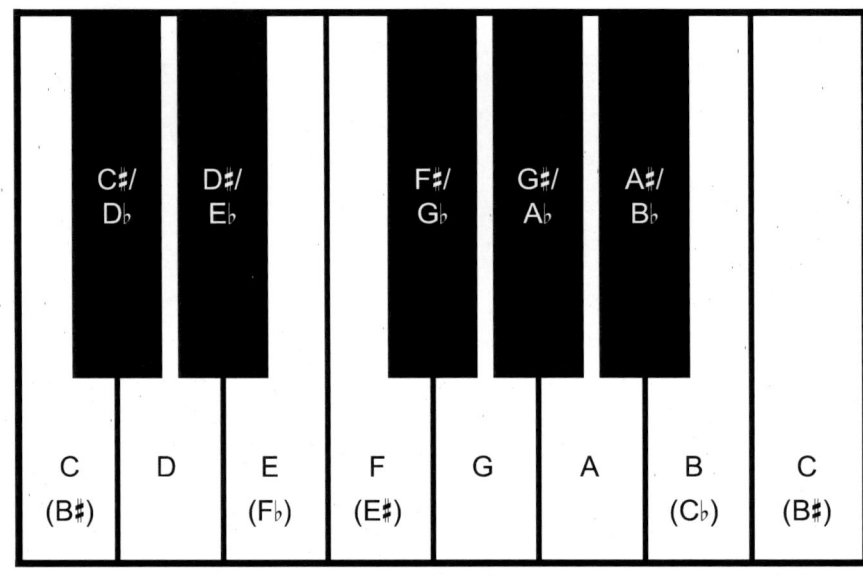

As an example, when the black key "G♯" is played, it sounds the same pitch as if it were played as "A♭". In other words, G♯=A♭.

The following diagram shows some enharmonic notes on the staff:

Same Pitch   Same Pitch   Same Pitch   Same Pitch   Same Pitch   Same Pitch

Lesson 11
Intervals

An **interval** is the distance in pitch between two notes. Intervals are made up of **half-steps** and **whole-steps**. Two half-steps make one whole-step. Picture a piano keyboard: the distance between each key on the piano is one half-step (this includes both white and black keys).

Intervals are assigned specific **numbers**. This number is found by counting upwards from the lower note, counting that note as the first. For example, an interval spanning from C to E is a third (C, D, E... 1, 2, 3). An interval that is two of the same note in the same position on the staff is called a **unison** instead of a first. An interval that spans eight notes is called an **octave**.

Intervals also have a specific **quality**. The possible qualities of an interval are **perfect**, **major**, **minor**, **augmented**, or **diminished**.

The following intervals are **perfect**: unison, 4th, 5th, octave

The following intervals are **major** or **minor**: 2nd, 3rd, 6th, 7th

The difference between a major and a minor interval with the same number name is that the major interval is one half-step wider than the minor interval.

An **augmented** interval is a major or perfect interval plus one half-step. A **diminished** interval is a minor or perfect interval minus one half-step. Two commonly used augmented and diminished intervals are the augmented fourth (perfect 4th plus one half-step) and the diminished fifth (perfect 5th minus one half-step). The augmented 4th and diminished 5th sound the same (they contain the same number of total half-steps), but are spelled differently, making them **enharmonic intervals**. These two intervals are known as **tritones** and contain three whole steps, also known as tones. A tritone is exactly one-half the intervallic value of one octave.

For reference, below is a list of the number of half-steps that comprise each interval. Use this information to determine the intervals between different notes by counting how many half steps are between them.

Minor 2nd: one half-step
Major 2nd: two half-steps
Minor 3rd: three half-steps
Major 3rd: four half-steps
Perfect 4th: five half-steps
Augmented 4th: six half-steps
Diminished 5th: six half-steps

Perfect 5th: seven half-steps
Minor 6th: eight half-steps
Major 6th: nine half-steps
Minor 7th: ten half-steps
Major 7th: eleven half-steps
Octave: twelve half-steps

The following example spells out the intervals introduced on the previous page, building upwards from middle C. They are shown both **melodically** (consecutive notes) and **harmonically** (notes played simultaneously, or stacked) on the staff.

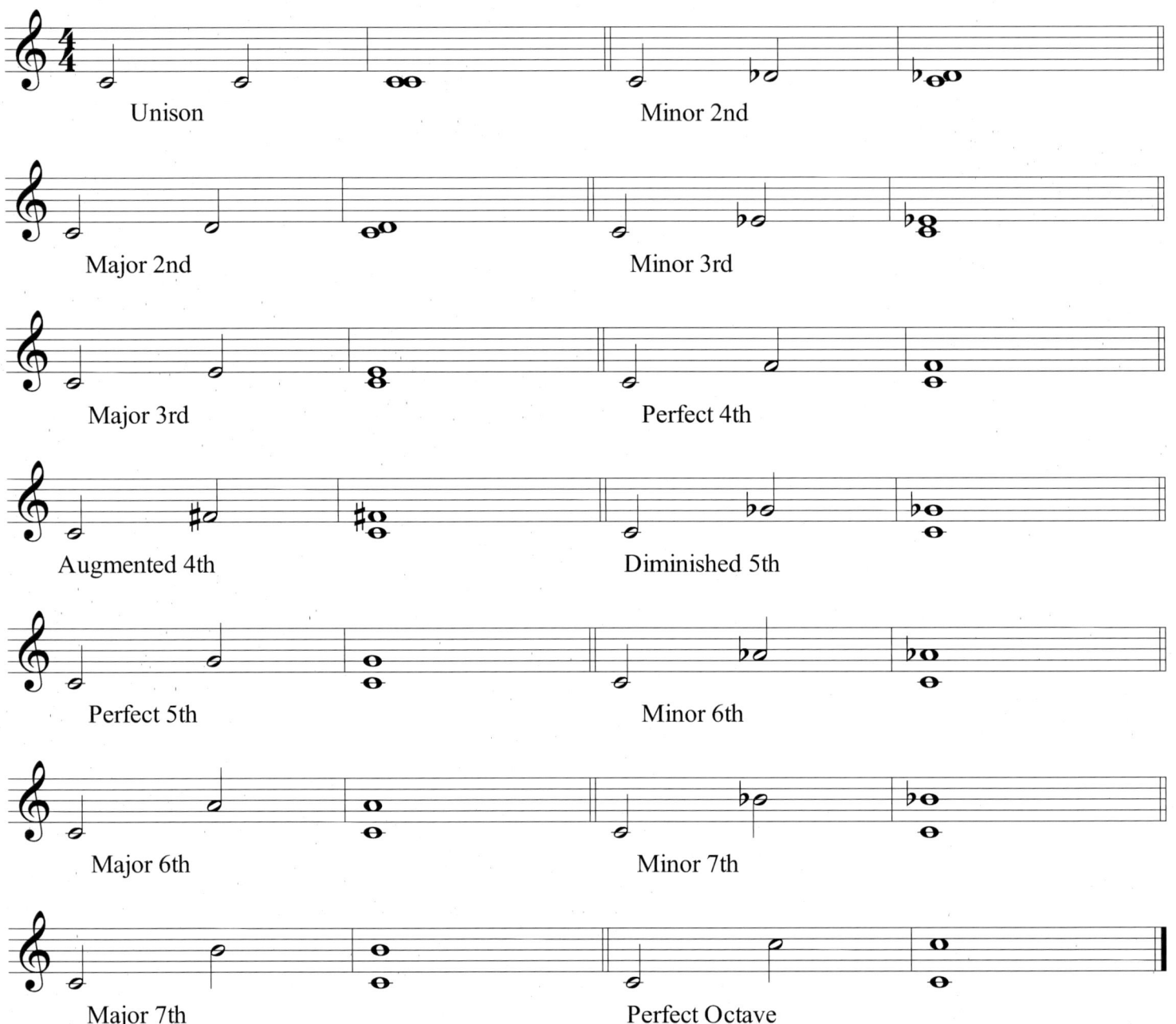

Lesson 12
Order of Sharps and Flats

Sharps and flats are added to a key signature in a certain order and always have the same placement on the staff.

Order of Sharps: F C G D A E B

One way to remember the order of sharps is to learn the following phrase:
"**F**at **C**ats **G**ood **D**ogs **A**lways **E**at **B**ologna"

The order of flats is the reverse of the order of sharps.

Order of Flats: B E A D G C F

To remember the order of flats, memorize the following:
The word "**BEAD**" followed by the math term "**G**reatest **C**ommon **F**actor", or "**GCF**".

These phrases are just examples. Feel free to come up with your own phrases to remember the order of sharps and flats.

Lesson 13
Major Keys

The diagrams below present the **major keys** according to the order of sharps and flats.

C Major and Sharp Keys:

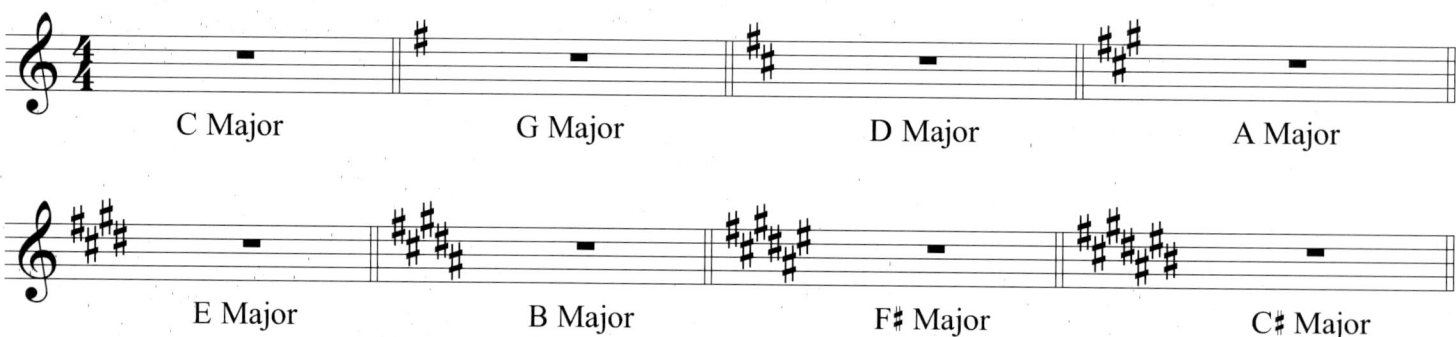

A trick for figuring out the name of a sharp key is to look at the sharp farthest to the right in the key signature and go up one letter name–this is the name of the key. For example, if the key signature has two sharps, the sharp furthest to the right is C♯. Go up one letter name and you will have D major. If this letter already has a sharp in the key signature, then there is a sharp in the name of the key (example: F♯ Major).

Flat Keys:

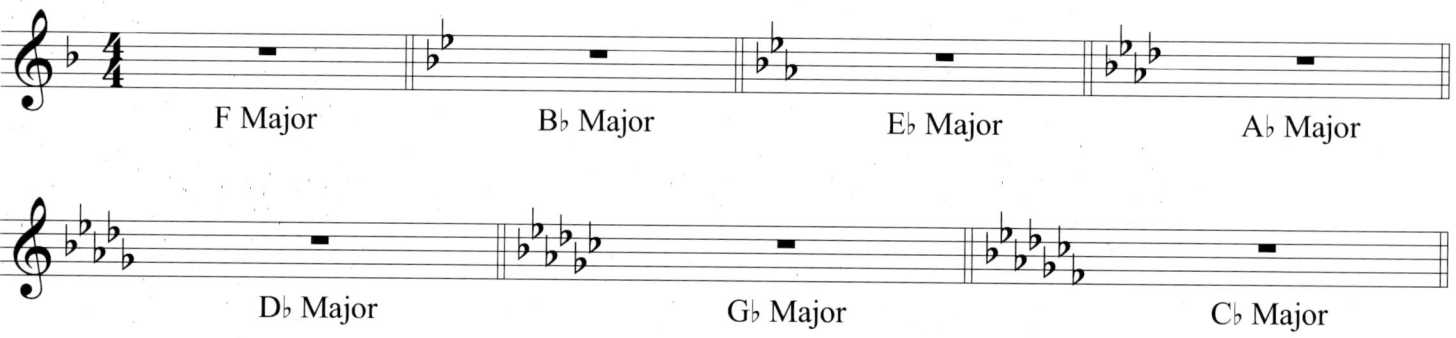

A way to determine the name of a flat key is to find the flat farthest to the right in the key signature and go back one flat to the left; this is the name of the key. This key will include the word "flat" in its name because the flat for the letter name is already in the key signature. As an example, if a key signature has two flats, the flat furthest to the right is E flat. Go to the left one flat for B flat and therefore B flat major. This trick only works for key signatures with more than one flat; memorize that F Major has one flat.

Lesson 14
Scale Degrees

A **scale** is a series of notes in order by tone, or pitch. Notes are assigned names and numbers that describe their place in a scale relative to other pitches, which makes talking about them clearer. There are several different systems for naming the notes in a scale. It is good to be familiar with all of these systems. Labeling notes in this way will be particularly helpful when learning about chords later in this book.

One way to classify notes in the scale is to assign them a **scale degree**. The scale degree is a number from 1 to 7 that describes a note's position in the scale. A scale degree number is usually paired with a caret symbol. In the example below, the position of each note in the one octave C Major scale is labeled with scale degree numbers. The key of C Major has no sharps or flats in its key signature.

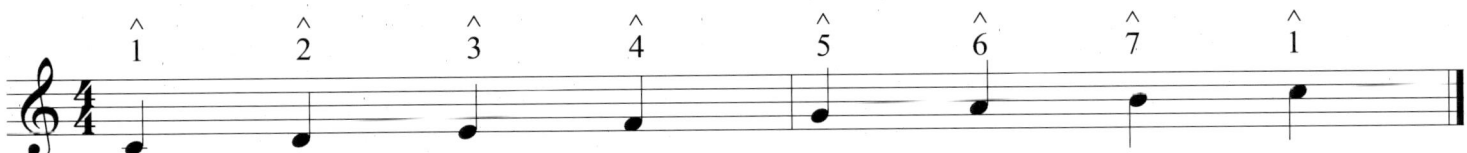

Sometimes scale degrees are labeled with syllables from the Solfège technique, which is frequently used for singing. Although we will not use Solfège labeling in this book, it is good to be familiar with these terms as well.

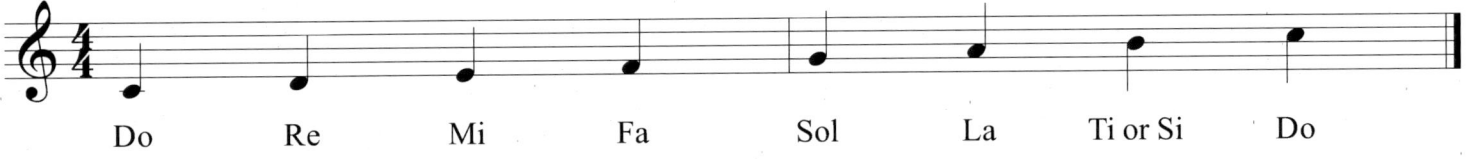

Finally, in addition to having a number or syllable, each scale degree has a name. These names will be important to know when learning about chords later on. Study the names of the scale degrees below.

1 tonic
2 supertonic
3 mediant
4 subdominant
5 dominant
6 submediant
7 subtonic (when there is a whole step between 7 and 1)
or **leading tone** (when there is a half step between 7 and 1)

Scale degrees identify the place of a note in a scale and not a specific note name, so they change according to the key. Scale degree 1, or tonic, in the key of C Major is the note C, but in the key of D Major, the tonic pitch is the note D.

Lesson 15
Major Scale

Remember that a **scale** is a sequence of notes in pitch order (see lesson 14). There are different kinds of scales, and the type of scale is defined by the placement of whole and half steps within the scale. In this lesson we will learn the **major scale**.

The major scale begins on scale degree 1, or tonic. The intervals that define the scale as major are two half-steps, between scale degrees 3 and 4 and again between 7 and 1. The pattern of whole and half steps in a major scale is WWHWWWH. So far we have seen a one-octave scale, but scales can span any number of octaves. Below is a two-octave scale in the key of D Major, ascending and descending. The half-step intervals are marked; all of the other intervals between notes are whole steps.

D Major:

Now compare the previous example to the next scale in E Major. The half-steps are in the same position as in the D major scale, but the notes and key are different.

E Major:

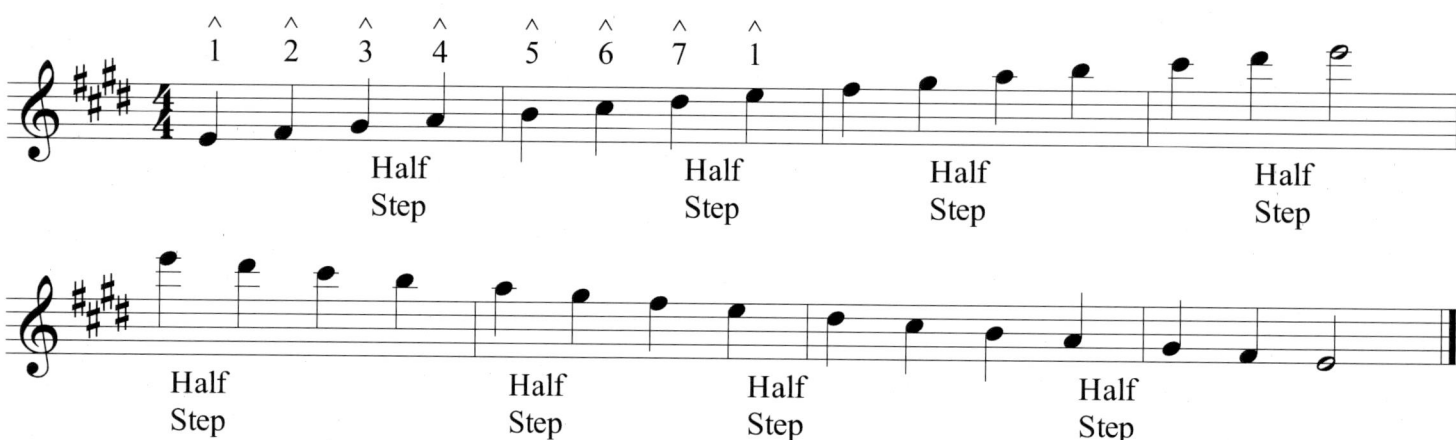

Lesson 16
Triplets

A **triplet** is three notes fit evenly into the space of two of the same kind of note. The triplet is marked with the number 3 and its three notes are sometimes connected with a bracket.

In 4/4 time, an eighth note triplet is three eighth notes fit into the same amount of time as two eighth notes, or one quarter note. Clap the following example, saying "ap-ple" for eighth notes and "tri-ple-it" for triplets, feeling how each fits into one beat.

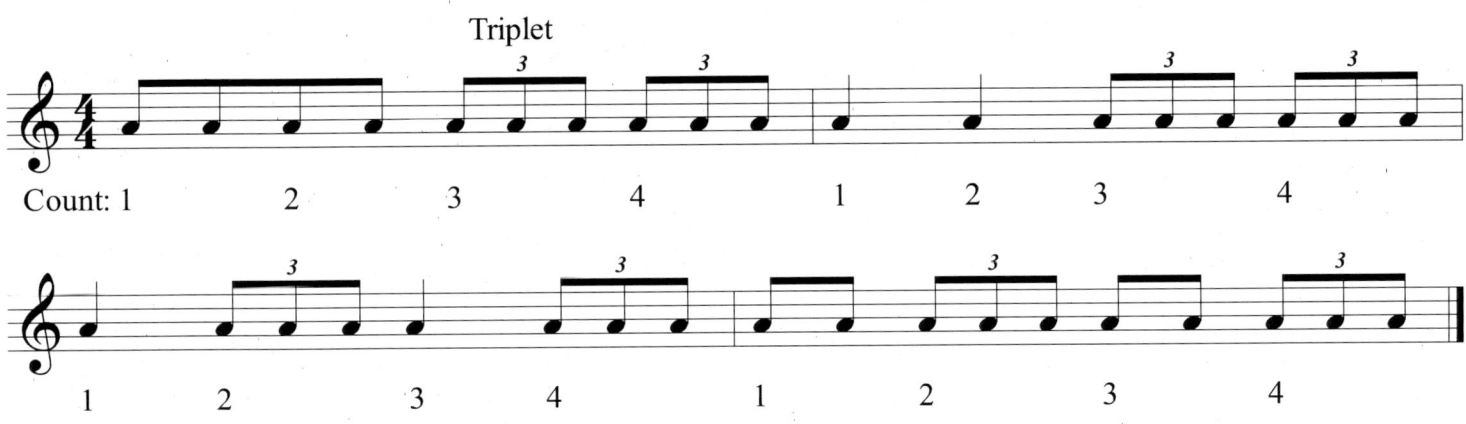

Similarly, a quarter note triplet is three quarter notes fit into the space of two quarter notes, or one half note. Counting now becomes more complicated: the quarter note triplets occur over two beats, so you must fit three quarter notes into 2 beats and the beats will not match up with the notes.

Lesson 17
Dynamics and Articulations

The term **dynamics** describes the volume of music. Dynamic markings are usually found at the beginning of a piece of music and often change throughout. Here are some of the most common dynamic indicators found in music:

ff *fortissimo*, very loud   *f* *forte*, loud   *mf* *mezzo-forte*, medium-loud
mp *mezzo-piano*, medium-soft   *p* *piano*, soft   *pp* *pianissimo*, very soft

Crescendo means to become gradually louder and can also be shown by the abbreviation *cresc.* or an opening hairpin symbol. *Decrescendo* means to become gradually softer and is often shown by the abbreviation *decresc.* or a closing hairpin symbol.

Articulations are markings that describe with what qualities to play or sing a note. There are many different possible articulations in music; here, we will explore **slurs**, **ties**, **accents**, and **staccato** markings.

A **slur** connects two or more notes and indicates that they should be played or sung **legato**, or smoothly. A **tie** is a slur that connects notes of the same pitch and indicates that there should be no re-articulation, or break, between the notes.

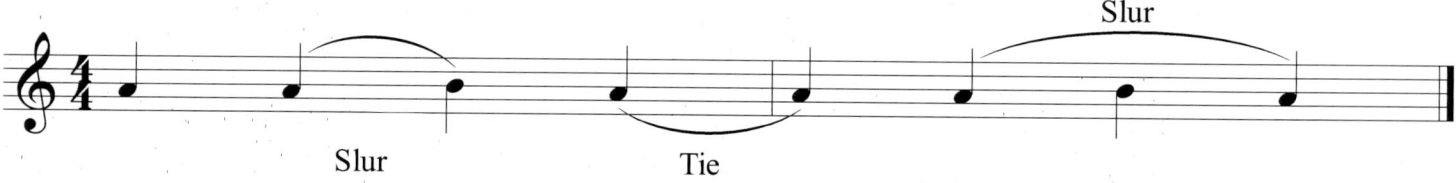

An **accent** is a wedge symbol above or below a note that means to emphasize the note with a sharp attack.

Staccato indicates that a note should be played short and separate. Staccato markings are small dots placed above or below notes.

Lesson 18
Repeats

Often all or part of a piece of music will be played or sung more than one time. This direction is written as a **repeat sign**, which is a double bar with two dots next to it. Repeat signs can face either forward or backward. When you encounter a repeat sign, return to the beginning of the music. If there is a more recent forward-facing repeat sign, start from that sign and play the section of music again.

When a piece of music has a repeated section that changes slightly at the end of the second time it is played, it is written with **first and second endings**. These are marked with a bracket and either the number 1 or 2. When playing the music the first time, play through the bracketed first ending to the repeat sign, then go back to the beginning or the previous repeat sign as with a regular repeat. The second time through, skip over the measures of the first ending and proceed to the second ending.

Lesson 19
More Time Signatures

In this lesson we will explore some new time signatures: **3/8, 6/8, 9/8**, and **12/8**.

In **3/8 time**, there are three 8th notes in a measure and the 8th note gets the beat. In this time signature, or **meter** (another term for time signature), as well as the others on this page, you can count the beats in eighth notes or feel a **pulse** on the first of each group of three eighth notes. In 3/8 time, the pulse is a dotted quarter note.

3 beats   pulse unit

In **6/8 time**, there are six 8th notes in a measure and the 8th note gets the beat. The pulse of this meter can be felt as two dotted quarter notes, which each contain three 8th notes.

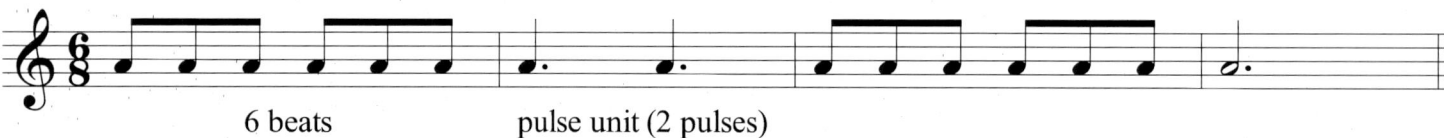

6 beats   pulse unit (2 pulses)

9/8 time has nine 8th notes in a measure and the 8th note gets the beat. The pulse of this meter can be felt as three dotted quarter notes, each containing three 8th notes. Count the dotted half note as six 8th notes.

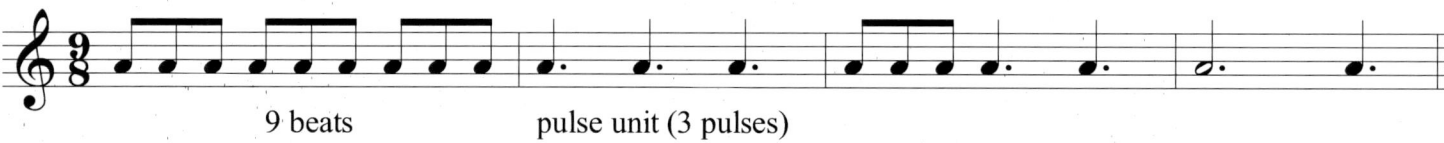

9 beats   pulse unit (3 pulses)

Following this pattern, the **12/8** time signature has twelve 8th notes in a measure and the 8th note gets the beat. The pulse of this meter can be felt as four dotted quarter notes, each containing three 8th notes.

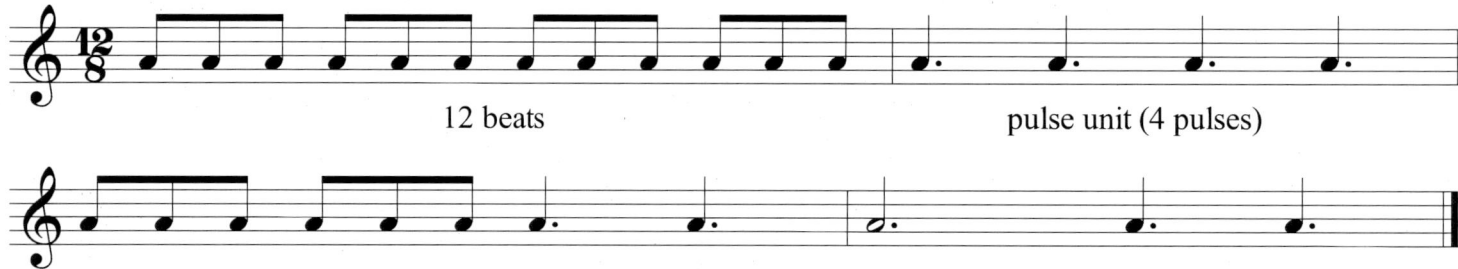

12 beats   pulse unit (4 pulses)

Lesson 20
Tempo

Tempo is a term that describes the speed of music. Tempo markings often appear at the beginning of a piece of music and may change throughout.

There are many possible terms used to indicate the tempo. Below are some of the more common terms:

Slow: *Lento (40), Largo (45), Adagio (55)*   Moderate: *Andante (75), Moderato (100)*
Fast: *Allegro (110), Vivace (140), Presto (170)*

There are also terms that mean that the tempo should speed up or slow down. Here are some of the most commonly used terms and their definitions:

ritardando (also *ritard.* or *rit.*): gradually slow down
meno mosso: slower (less motion)
accelerando (also *accel.*): gradually speed up
più mosso: faster (more motion)
a tempo: return to the previous tempo

In the following exercise, try clapping all of the various tempo indications and changes, using a metronome and the beats-per-minute markings above.

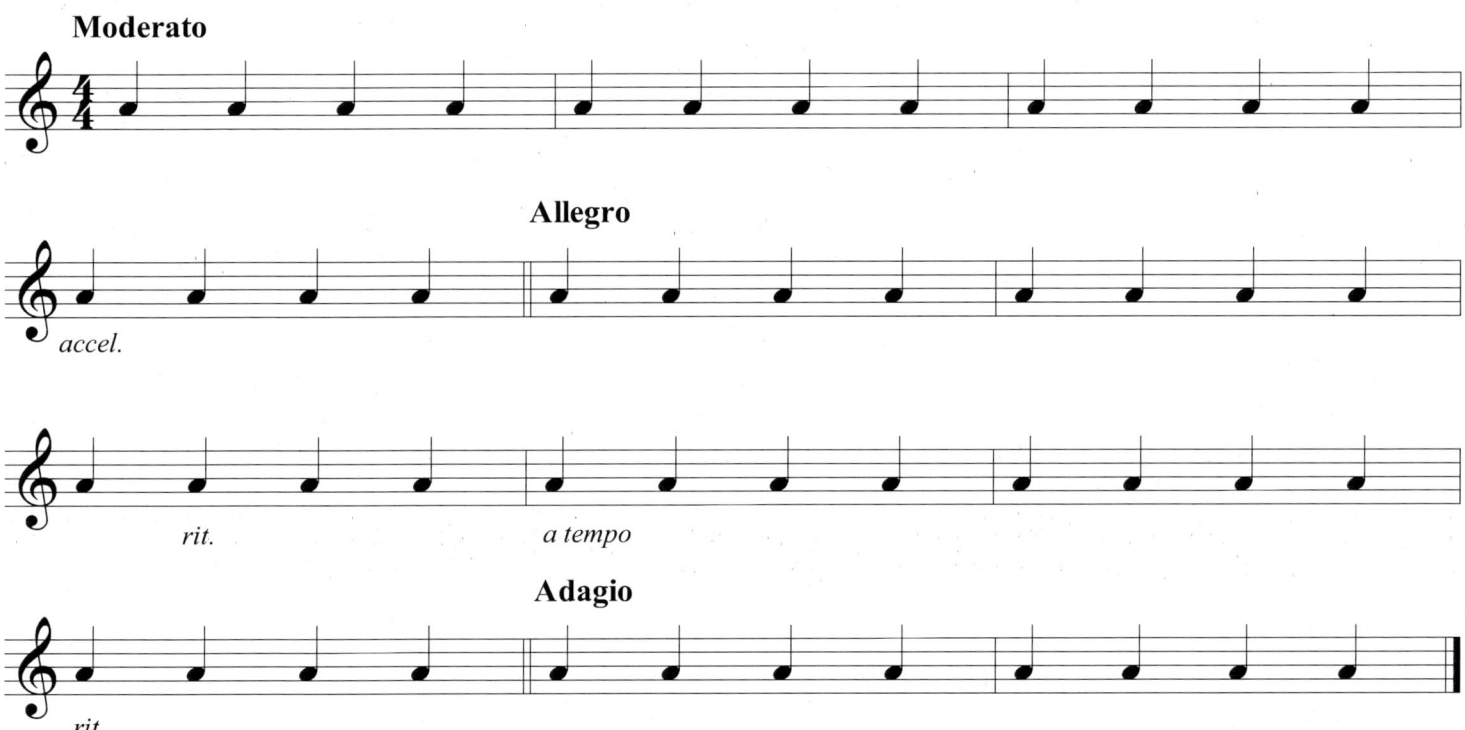

Lesson 21
Minor Keys

Every major key has a **relative minor** key that shares the same key signature. The name of the relative minor key is the letter name one third below the name of the relative major key (scale degree 6). So, for example, with the key of C major, go down a 3rd to arrive at its relative minor, the key of A minor. Practice finding the relative minor of each major key until you have memorized them.

The diagrams below present the minor keys according to the order of sharps and flats, with their relative major keys in parentheses. Minor key names typically use lowercase letters.

A minor and Sharp Keys:

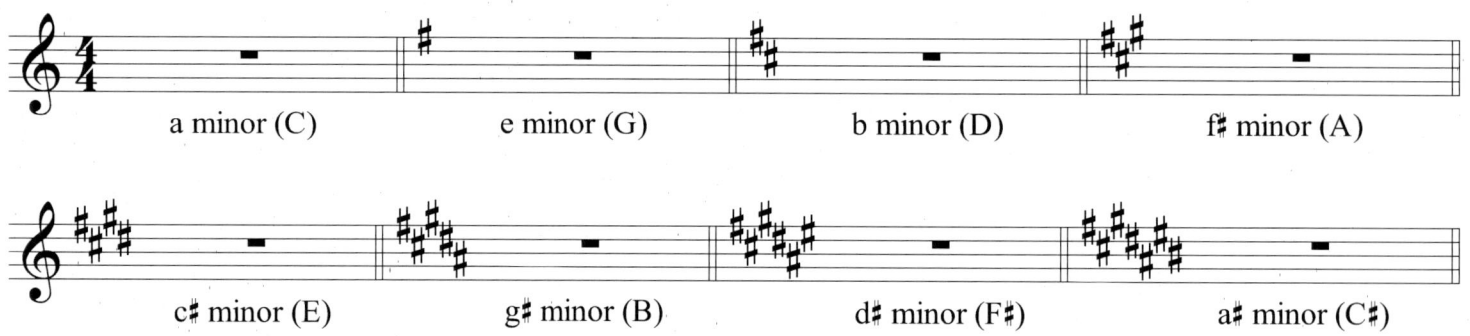

Flat Keys:

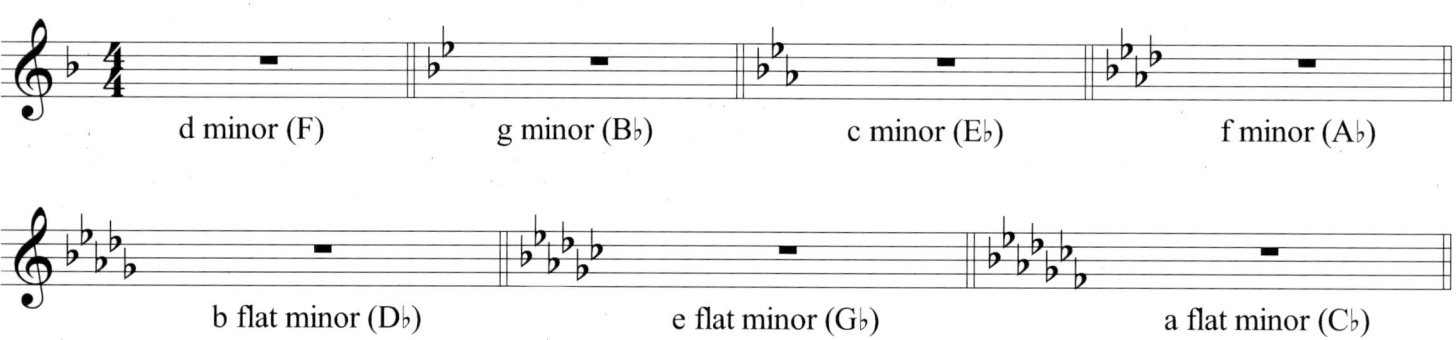

Lesson 22
Minor Scales

The primary difference between a major scale and a **minor scale** is the interval between scale degrees 1 and 3. In the major scale, this interval is a *major* 3rd, but in the minor scale, scale degree 3 is lowered by one half-step and the resulting interval is a *minor* 3rd.

There are three different kinds of minor scales: **melodic minor**, **natural minor**, and **harmonic minor**. The difference between the scales has to do with the placement of half-steps within the scale.

The **natural minor scale** has all of the same notes as its relative major scale. Its tonic is scale degree 6 of the relative major. There are two half-steps in the natural minor scale: between scale degrees 2 and 3 and also 5 and 6. This scale is the same ascending and descending.

Natural minor scale in A minor:

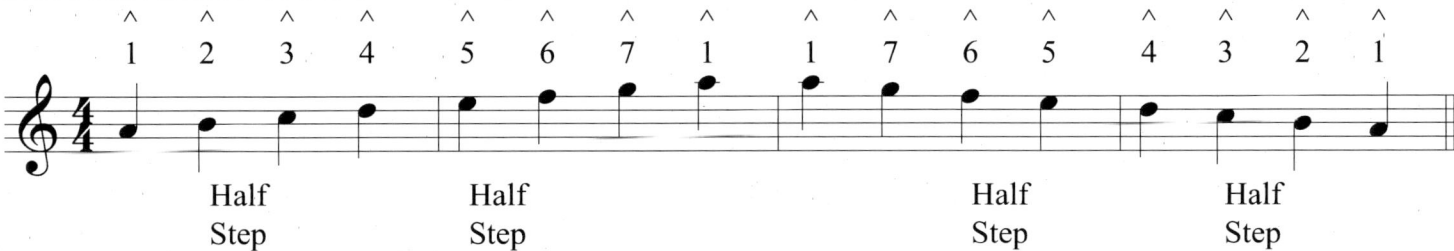

The **harmonic minor scale** differs from the natural minor scale in that scale degree 7 is one half-step higher. When scale degree 7 is raised, it is known as the **leading tone** because it "leads" to the tonic pitch. This scale has three half-steps and is the same ascending and descending.

Harmonic minor scale in A minor:

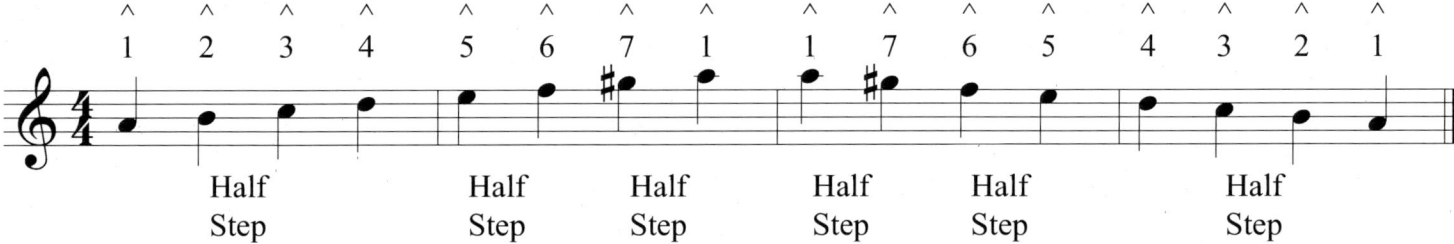

The **melodic minor scale** has different notes when ascending than it does when descending. The ascending melodic minor scale has raised scale degrees 6 and 7 (each by a half-step), creating an augmented 2nd between these two pitches. The descending scale is the same as the descending natural minor scale, so scale degrees 6 and 7 are lowered by one half-step from the ascending scale.

Melodic minor scale in A minor:

Lesson 23
Triads

A **chord** is a group of three or more notes played at the same time. A **triad** is a type of chord that consists of three notes, each a third apart. The bottom note of a triad is called the **root**, and the middle and top notes are called the **third** and **fifth**, respectively. The interval from the bottom to the middle note is a third and from the bottom to the top is a fifth.

Like intervals, triads can be major, minor, augmented, or diminished. The quality of the triad changes depending on the qualities of the intervals between notes in the triad.

Building from the root:
Major triad: major 3rd, perfect 5th (major 3rd plus minor 3rd)
Minor triad: minor 3rd, perfect 5th (minor 3rd plus major 3rd)
Augmented triad: major 3rd, augmented 5th (major 3rd plus major 3rd)
Diminished triad: minor 3rd, diminished 5th (minor 3rd plus minor 3rd)

Below are the above-mentioned types of triads built on the pitch C.

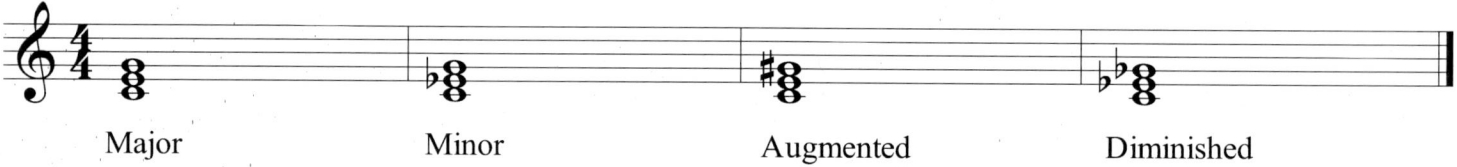

Major   Minor   Augmented   Diminished

Within a scale, triads can be built on any scale degree. In major and minor scales, these triads will have different qualities depending on which scale degree they are built. The triads built on the notes of the scale adhere to the key signature of the scale and are named with Roman numerals, using upper case letters for major triads and lower case letters for minor triads. Augmented chords are indicated by a small plus sign next to the Roman numeral, and diminished chords by a small circle.

Sometimes triads are referred to by the letter name of the root followed by the quality of the triad. For a major chord, the letter name appears alone. For a minor chord, the letter name, which is sometimes lowercase, is followed by a lowercase "m".

In a major scale, the pattern for the qualities of the triads built on each scale degree is:
I–ii–iii–IV–V–vi–vii°.
1 2 3 4 5 6 7
Major–minor–minor–Major–Major–minor–diminished

Triads in C Major:

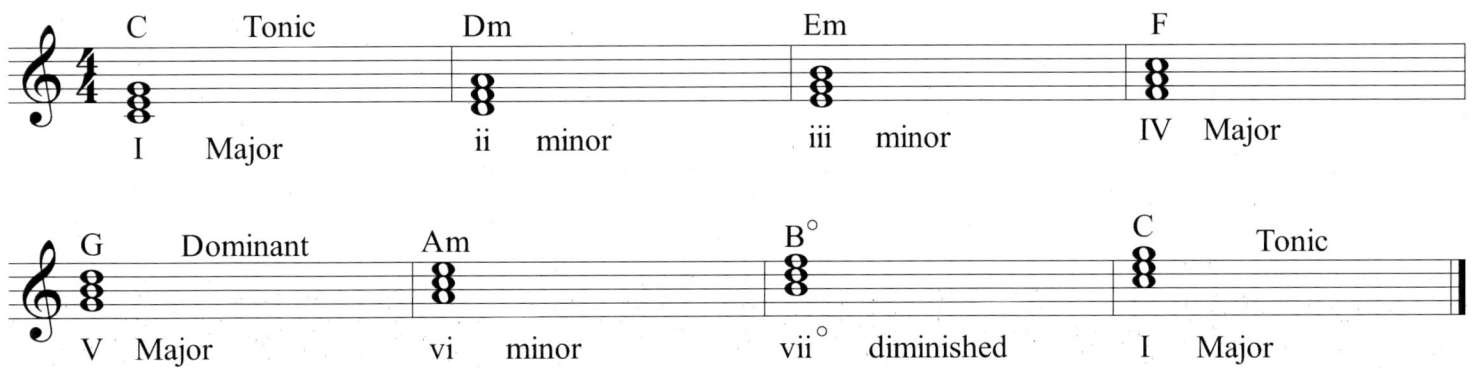

In the natural minor scale, the pattern for the qualities of the triads is:
i–ii°–III–iv–v–VI–VII
1 2 3 4 5 6 7
minor–diminished–Major–minor–minor–Major–Major

Triads in A natural minor:

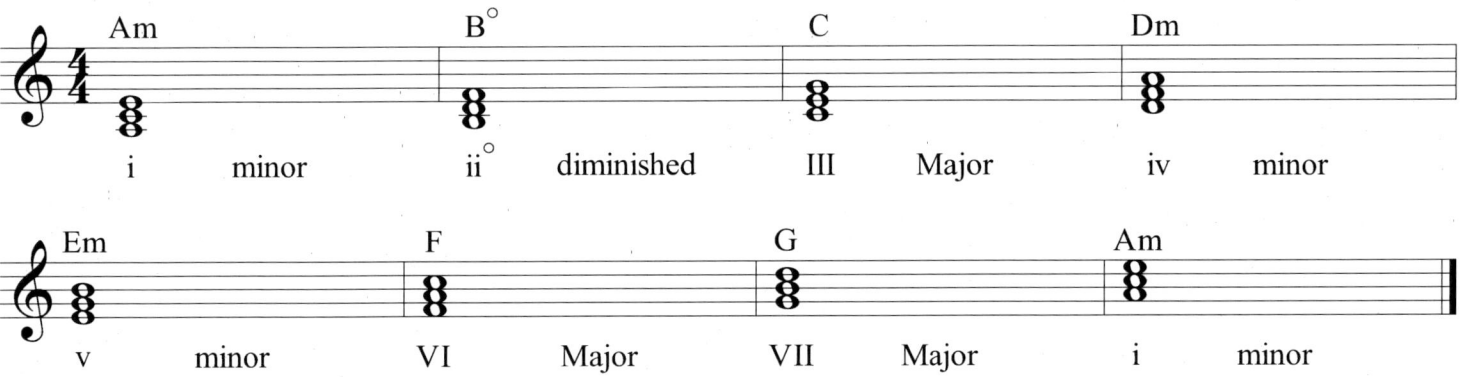

Lesson 24
Arpeggios

An **arpeggio** is the notes of a chord played melodically (separately) instead of simultaneously as with a chord. When a chord is written out melodically, it is **arpeggiated**.

Arpeggiated C major tonic triad:

Along with scales, arpeggios are a commonly used technical exercise for most musicians. Below are a major and minor scale followed by their respective arpeggios.

D Major one-octave scale and arpeggio:

B (natural) minor one-octave scale and arpeggio:

Lesson 25
Inversions

Triads can be written with their notes in different orders; in other words, a note other than the root can appear as the lowest note of the chord. These are called **inversions**.

The triads we have already seen are in **root position**, which means that the root is the lowest note in the triad. Sometimes there are numbers written next to the Roman numeral name of the triad. These numbers are called **figured bass** and are a way of explaining what intervals are in the triad. In a root position tonic triad, the figured bass will be I 5–3. The 5 signifies the 5th above the root and the 3 signifies the 3rd above the root.

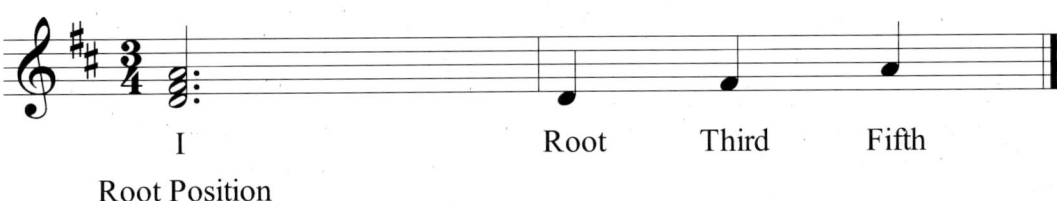

In a **first inversion** triad, the root is moved to the top of the chord, and thus the 3rd becomes the bottom note. The figured bass for the 1st inversion triad is 6–3 and is commonly written just as 6. The number 6 indicates that there is now an interval of a 6th between the bottom note (the 3rd) and the top note (the repositioned root).

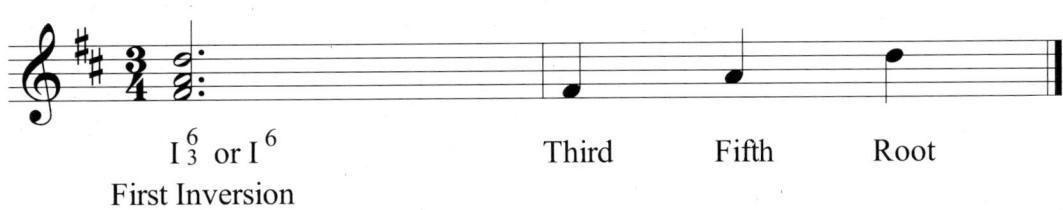

In a **second inversion** triad, the original third is moved to the top of the chord, the root is in its raised position as in first inversion, and the fifth becomes the bottom note. Now the order from the lowest note is fifth, root, third. The figured bass for the 2nd inversion triad is 6–4, which indicates that there is a 6th between the bottom note (5th) and top note (3rd) and a 4th between the bottom note and center note (root).

Lesson 26
Seventh Chords

Another common type of chord is the **seventh chord**, which is a triad with an additional third added on top. This creates an interval of a 7th between the root of the chord and the top note. There are several different kinds of seventh chords, and they have different names depending on the quality of the triad and of the seventh above the root.

Dominant 7th: major triad, minor 7th (between root and 7th). This is the most common 7th chord; it is called a **major–minor 7th** when it is based on any scale degree except scale degree 5.
Major 7th: major triad, major 7th
Minor 7th: minor triad, minor 7th
Half-diminished 7th: diminished triad, minor 7th
Diminished 7th (also called fully-diminished): diminished triad, diminished 7th

Below are the first four of the above-mentioned seventh chords, built on C. Note the shorthand names for each kind of seventh chord written above each chord. Root position seventh chords are indicated by a Roman numeral with the superscript 7. Remember that a dominant 7 is built on scale degree 5. Here, the chord in the first measure is a major–minor seventh chord because it is built on C. The dominant seventh chord in the following measure has G, scale degree 5 in C major, as its root. The two chords contain the same intervals.

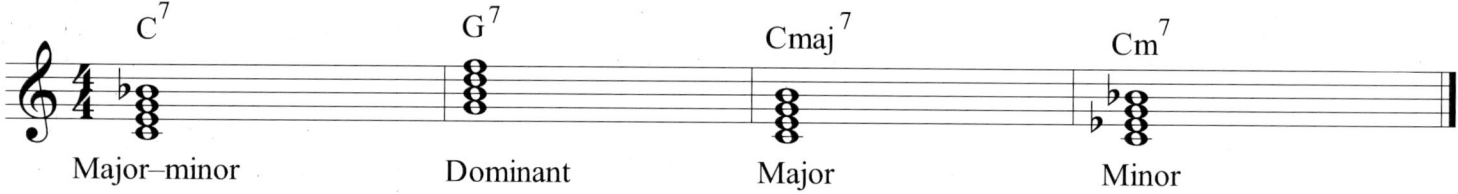

Now let's examine the half-diminished and diminished seventh chords. These chords introduce some new symbols. A half-diminished chord is signified by a diminished symbol with a slash through it. In the diminished 7th chord below, in order to make the 7th on top of the root a diminished 7th we must **double flat** the note B, making it enharmonic with A. This is written just how you might expect: by two flat symbols right next to each other.

Just like with triads, one can invert 7th chords. As discussed on the previous page, **root position** seventh chords have a Roman numeral label and a superscript 7. As with a triad, the root is the lowest note, followed by the 3rd, 5th, and 7th.

Root position:

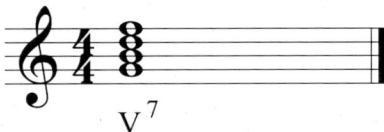

In a **first inversion** seventh chord, the root moves to the top of the chord and the third becomes the lowest note, or **bass**. The intervals above the bass (the third) are 6, 5, and 3 (6–5–3) and the figured bass is abbreviated 6–5 (the 3 is omitted). Numbers are omitted from figured bass because only the characteristic/unique intervals of the inversions are indicated.

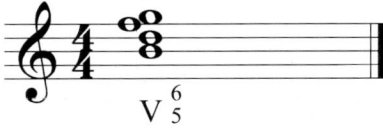

The **second inversion** seventh chord has the fifth in the bass with the third moved to the top. This creates intervals of 6, 4, and 3 (6–4–3) over the fifth in the bass with figured bass abbreviated as 4–3.

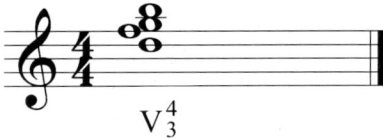

Third inversion seventh chords have the seventh as the bass with the fifth moved to the top. The intervals over the bass are 6, 4, and 2 (6–4–2), abbreviated 4–2.

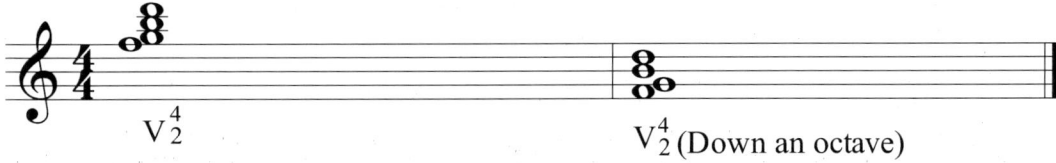